T0349353

Elementary Particles

Elementary Particles

Sneha Madhavan-Reese

Brick Books

Library and Archives Canada Cataloguing in Publication

Title: Elementary particles / Sneha Madhavan-Reese.
Names: Madhavan-Reese, Sneha, author.
Description: Poems.
Identifiers: Canadiana (print) 2023046551X | Canadiana (ebook) 20230465544 |
ISBN 9781771316194 (softcover) | ISBN 9781771316200 (EPUB) | ISBN 9781771316217 (PDF)
Classification: LCC PS8626.A31755 E44 2023 | DDC C811/.6—dc23

Copyright © Sneha Madhavan-Reese, 2023

We gratefully acknowledge the Canada Council for the Arts, the Government of Canada through the Canada Book Fund, and the Ontario Arts Council for their support of our publishing program.

Canada Council   Conseil des arts
for the Arts   du Canada

ONTARIO ARTS COUNCIL
CONSEIL DES ARTS DE L'ONTARIO
an Ontario government agency
un organisme du gouvernement de l'Ontario

Government   Gouvernement
of Canada   du Canada

Edited by Cara-Lyn Morgan.

The cover image is a photograph of particle tracks in a bubble chamber, courtesy of CERN.
Author photo by Sara McConnell.
The book is set in FreightText Pro and Berthold Akzidenz Grotesk.
Design by Emma Allain.
Printed and bound by Coach House Printing.

Brick Books
487 King St. W.
Kingston, ON
K7L 2X7
www.brickbooks.ca

lb
BRICK BOOKS

Though much of the work of Brick Books takes place on the ancestral lands of the Anishinaabeg, Haudenosaunee, Huron-Wendat, and Mississaugas of the Credit peoples, our editors, authors, and readers from many backgrounds are situated from coast to coast to coast in Canada on the traditional and unceded territories of over six hundred nations who have cared for Turtle Island from time immemorial. While living and working on these lands, we are committed to hearing and returning the rightful imaginative space to the poetries, songs, and stories that have been untold, under-told, wrongly told, and suppressed through colonization.

for my family

Hold fast.
You are not yet the person
you will be.
–Carole Glasser Langille

CONTENTS

Elementary Particles

1.

The smallest—as-of-yet indivisible—
building blocks of everything, fermions

form the matter around us and bosons
carry interactions between them.

We named the atom from the Greek *atomos*,
meaning "uncut." Later we learned of the nucleus,

bound by the strongest force (strong beyond
our imagination—we could only call it *strong*),

like a liquid drop or arrangement of energy shells,
and capable of transformation. It splits.

Its nucleons split again.

2.

All elementary particles are manifestations
of a conserved energy. There are universal laws:

Heat or work or mass must move
to keep systems in equilibrium.

Also, once done, things cannot be undone
without loss.

3.

Quarks decay: up to down, top to bottom, charm to strange.
The Higgs boson, when we finally found it, left

only traces of its existence: W and Z bosons, a tau-antitau pair.
We observe fields by measuring perturbations.

In the kinetic unrest of the solar core, two protons collide.
For fusion to ensue, a single quark must transform. The power

vital for life on Earth is unleashed by a force we call *weak*.
We seek solutions by breaking things apart.

4.

Archimedes used myriads, from the Greek *myrias*,
the number ten thousand, to count the grains

of sand to fill the universe. His body in the bathtub
to find the density of adulterated gold.

Everyday matter, sand and water,
moves through space as particles and waves.

Archimedes anticipated modern mathematics.
He reduced the void to infinitesimals.

5.

Amber, when rubbed with a piece of dry cloth,
attracts feathers or bits of torn paper.

A jar filled with water and holding a brass rod
stores energy when held in the hand.

Cathode rays cast shadows. Magnets
bend luminescent beams. Oil droplets,

in a fine mist, charged through friction
with a sprayer nozzle, defy gravity.

The Greek word for amber is *ēlektron*.

6.

The notion of *particle* is anything but
particular: certainty is subject

to fundamental limitations. We can know
the tiniest bits of our beings only as probabilities.

In the atoms of my fingertips, your hair, this chair:
quarks, antiquarks, and gluons wink

in and out of being. Our bodies are built
of ephemera. We exist in dynamic equilibria.

7.

Dirac puzzled over a new description
of the electron. His relativistic wave equation yielded

negative-energy solutions. Guided by theory alone,
Dirac postulated the positron.

Every particle of matter
has a corresponding particle of antimatter.

If they should meet—
mutual annihilation in a photon flash.

8.

In the beginning, space and time burst into being,
dense and energetic. A hot chaos for creation

and destruction, matter
and antimatter in equal parts, at least

it should have been. What carried this asymmetry
to create this place we occupy?

Extrapolate backwards to a primordial singularity.
We approach but never arrive at the unknowable.

9.

In the beginning, we placed a flat Earth
at the centre of a cosmic sea. We named

the elements: earth, water, air, fire, and aether.

We set a spherical Earth at the centre of the universe
and commanded the sun and planets to revolve around it.

We decided to orbit the sun. We replaced the edge
of the universe with star-filled space. We realized

we were nowhere near the centre.

10.

The Greek *kosmos* means "order," especially
"the arrangement of troops for battle"

—our world consists of energy we divide and control—

but is also the root of *cosmetic*. Our universe is beautiful,
but superficial. All particles we call *real*,

we understand as excitations.

11.

What we call a vacuum is full
of random fluctuations, transient

pairs of virtual particles. The truly fundamental

are not particles at all. What we call an electron
is a quantum of the electron field. What, then,

is a field? Could a fish describe water?

Could a moth explain the inside of its cocoon,
as its tissues dissolve and reimagine themselves?

12.

In the beginning, we quarrelled over dichotomies:
black and white, matter and light. Seeking the smallest,

we split and outgrew our own solid bodies.
Seeking truth, we discovered faith in uncertainty.

From the churning centres of distant stars
to the fleeting inspirations of our human minds,

all particles arise from an underlying unity, continuous
across space and time. We are not separate, you and I.

Rosa Parks

The day her body was laid out for viewing,
I was getting nothing useful done, so I left
work early and drove downtown.
The line of people wound all around
the Museum of African American History.
I wouldn't get to see her: the wait
would be hours, I'd brought no coins
to feed a meter, and there was nowhere
else to park. A man approached
to offer me all the change in his pockets.
I'll always have fond memories of Detroit.

Mapping

I was raised near the jutting-out
knuckle on the thumb of my right hand.
A native Michigander, I was never
without a map of the state, its lower peninsula
shaped like an open palm. My life line
traced the path of I-69. We took school field trips
to Lansing, in my palm's centre,
and vacationed at the tip of my pinky,
in the sands of the Sleeping Bear Dunes.

We went on longer trips to India
to visit my parents' relatives. In rural Kerala,
no one uses maps—our driver navigated unmarked roads
by calling out to locals from his window.
They told him, by landmark, where to take
a turn. Finally, my father recognized
the walled streets of his village, and from the road
he showed me the house where he was born, though
it wasn't in our family anymore. We couldn't drop in for tea.
In a clearing, women took nimble backward steps
as they spun coir rope from the fibres of coconut husks.
If he had never left this place, one of those women
would be me. Watching them work, I turned my palm
fingers down to map my father's hometown. Here it is,
in the first segment of my index finger, under
the thatched roofs of the Malabar Coast,
at the edge of the Arabian Sea.

Guruvayoor

Even before 3 a.m.
strings of fresh jasmine hang in their stalls,
thread looped and tied around

the base of each fragrant bud. I am walking
with my mother. It is dark, and even
if she didn't know the way, the way

is unmistakable. The road is filled
with people on foot, and lined with stalls
of flower-sellers. My mother buys a string for my hair.

When we arrive at the temple, the doors
are closed; we are early enough. We wait,
and the line grows behind us. But then

my mother steps aside, feeling faint,
she says. I'm to stay in line. She won't let me
go with her. She reminds me

that to be here in the morning is a blessing.
I stand barefoot among strangers.
All the women wear flowers in their hair.

Suddenly, the crowd pushes. I stumble
but don't fall. When I look up
we are face-to-face. The Lord is adorned

with flowers, gold chains, and coloured cloth,
ornaments from the day before. The priest
performs the morning prayers, then removes these jewels.

He pours on oil, then yellow-brown powder,
and washes the idol clean. The black stone gleams.
I walk through the temple clockwise

and touch my forehead to the floor. The sun
has not yet risen. Today's jasmine has not yet begun
to brown. I have seen the daily miracle

of the Lord's morning bath.
My mother will be satisfied.

Teachings

Before each semester began,
my father and I reviewed
his class list, and I taught him
how to pronounce the names
of all his students. For days,
he practiced shaping *Barbara*'s *r*'s
without tapping his tongue
to the roof of his mouth
and relaxing into *Pamela*'s subtle vowels,
so unlike the always articulated
syllables of his mother tongue.
He didn't need to prepare any lectures—
chemistry was his second nature—
but he repeated the names aloud to himself,
recorded his voice on tape
and played it back until he was satisfied
that he could take the first day's attendance.

To Thousand Island

The only time I tasted you
was in a fast food restaurant
on an elementary school field trip.
I heard myself saying your name,
only because the girl in front of me
had asked for you. Her name was Amy.
Amy was confident and popular, and
she knew about things like salad dressing.
I had never eaten a salad in my life. Our house
always smelled of Indian curries. I didn't know
the names of different dressings, even that there were
different dressings, or even that there were such things
as dressings. I was maybe eight; it was maybe grade three.
I don't remember where we were going, but I remember Amy's voice.
I listened carefully so I'd know just what to order. When you arrived,
orange and tangy, you tasted horrid, but I was happy.
Perhaps I could find my way in this world after all.

My *Ramayana*

It was in Hindi, a language we didn't speak or understand,
but my parents and I watched all seventy-eight episodes
on VHS tapes rented from the Indian grocer. The dialogue
didn't matter; I knew the story well. It's the classic Hindu
morality tale, the story of God incarnate as the perfect man: fair-skinned
Rama, heir to the throne, who left for exile to keep his father's word.

When his wife was kidnapped, he built a bridge across the ocean
with an army of monkeys and bears. He killed ten-headed Ravana
and rescued Sita, but couldn't take her back without a trial
by fire. He was the perfect husband, and also the perfect king.

The people of India are masters of deification.
When the actor who played Rama
walked along the street, devotees threw themselves at his feet.
He had to quit smoking due to public outcry.

I'd always been drawn to Rama's younger brother instead.
What kind of man would enslave himself, choose loyalty
above all else? At night, I'd lie awake and imagine
scenes that were never written, like Lakshmana's conversations
with Urmila, his wife: his telling her he'd be leaving
with his brother for fourteen years, the story of how he disfigured a woman
by cutting off her nose and ears, and how he wept
as he gathered the wood to burn her sister, Sita, alive.

Thoppil Bhasi

I didn't know any names for fruits in Malayalam,
and he didn't know them in English, so I ran
up and down the stairs with every kind of fruit we had.
We discovered it was strawberries he'd been wanting.

He was famous back in India,
a playwright, I thought, or a poet. It was 1989;
I was ten, and used to Indian celebrities—
movie stars and dancers—but this was the first
writer who stayed with us, as a guest of my father's club.
His thinning, white hair didn't hide his brown scalp.
Thick, black glasses framed his eyes.

I asked him to sign my autograph book,
and he covered a whole page with his native script,
blue ink on light pink paper. The bulbous letters
my father had taught me to read were a mystery of loops
in his fluent hand. I could make out only the top line,
the familiar characters of my name repeated twice:
Sneha-mulla Sneha-mol. Loving daughter Sneha.

Etymology

In Middle English, *gramarye*
encompassed all learning—
from reading, writing, and philology
to spells, astrology, and incantation.

From this root, we have *grammar*,
the dictates of language, and *glamour*,
derived from supernatural study,
its charm and allure
descendants of bewitchment.

Entire worlds—Alice's Wonderland,
Tolkien's Middle-earth—are conjured
through words' mysterious
medium. Words make wizards
of us all—even your using
a possessive before a gerund
is something akin
to magic.

Four

Is 4 the same 4 for everybody?
–Pablo Neruda, *The Book of Questions*

My mother draws her four with a right angle;
my father's is pointed on top. My daughter's four,
half the time, is backward. Her sister signs,
tucking a thumb into her raised palm.

"I just adore four," Big Bird sings, "the number
for me," on an old record, *old* meaning
from a time when every kid knew how to drop
a needle into a spinning vinyl groove.

Four forces govern all things in the universe.
Carbon's four valence electrons form the basis
for all life: our four limbs and four-chambered
hearts, a four-leafed clover's lucky leaves.

My father shows me how to write the number
four in Malayalam—*naalu*, a round house
with a curve of smoke escaping. He says
no one uses these characters anymore.

On the First Direct Detection of Gravitational Waves

In high school physics, gravity
caused objects to fall. It was the science
of ordinary things, books and pencils and simple
mathematics. An apple hit Isaac on the head. I built a machine
out of plywood, bolts, and string.

Then Einstein curved spacetime, and the earth began falling
along a geodesic. Mercury's perihelion, no longer
anomalous, precessed as equations predicted.
Our sun deflected starlight twice as far as before.

If two black holes collide but no one hears them,
do gravitational waves really exist? For one hundred years,
they were locked in non-linear field equations. Scientists
wrote proposals and studied prototypes, focused lasers
and measured noise. They built an observatory
with no telescope, but with vacuum tubes encased in concrete.
Weiss walked the tunnels' lengths and cleaned out wasp infestations.

Before multicellular life evolved on Earth,
two stellar-mass black holes circled each other
and coalesced. More than a billion years later, mirrors
polished to atomic precision
shifted less than one-thousandth the diameter of a proton.
Light beams travelled nearly seven hundred miles
before they met and interfered, and the resulting waveform
converted to pressure in air
was audible to humans. It sounded like a chirp.

Gravity still makes objects fall, but now we know
ripples in spacetime squeeze and stretch us all.

Professor Daniel S. Kemp

He chalked perfect hexagons
on the lecture hall's movable blackboards.
It was my first semester at MIT, my first days
away from home. Everything
enthralled me.

He arranged the different colours
between his left-hand fingers. As he spoke, he drew
molecules and their reactions, electron-pushing arrows,
every detail woven in narrative, every lecture
a measured performance.

From his obituary, decades later, I learned
that he loved Shakespeare. I might have known.
He crafted, out of organic chemistry, stories
as compelling as any played onstage. Each class held me
spellbound.

Taxicab Numbers

I remember going to see him once when he was lying ill in Putney. I had ridden in taxi-cab No. 1729, and remarked that the number seemed to me rather a dull one, and that I hoped that it was not an unfavourable omen. "No," he replied, "it is a very interesting number; it is the smallest number expressible as a sum of two cubes in two different ways."
–G. H. Hardy, on Srinivasa Ramanujan

There are even and odd,
perfect and prime, surreal,
superreal, and hyperreal.
They can be negative,
irrational, or imaginary. Even
transcendental, if they aren't
roots of non-zero polynomials
with rational coefficients.
My favourites are the figurates, numbers
with history and form. Pythagoras
drew triangles and pentagons
and shaped a new view of the universe.
His students worshipped numbers
as the world's creative force.

They may seem unfeeling
and dull, containing nothing
of *poetry*. But look
at Fibonacci numbers
in the leaves of a willow
and the petals of a delphinium,
their ratio in the spiralling
scales of a pinecone. See the power
of Euler's number manifest
in your investments, and know
that Apéry's constant lies deep within
the gyromagnetic ratio of every

infinitesimal electron, from
the surface of far-off Uranus
to the skin of your fingertips.

After Ramanujan's offhand,
sickbed remark, we now
have another set of numbers
that numbers can be. The next time
you ride in a taxi, see
whether its number can be written
as the sum of two cubes
in more than one way.
Thank mathematicians for poems
that come and stop at your door.

Galgo Sitting

They can reach thirty miles per hour
in seconds, my neighbour tells me. She's watched
greyhounds for years. She's nervous, though,
because this dog knows only Spanish,
and she speaks only a few words.
Be good to him, the owner has warned.
If he thinks you're mad, he won't come back.

She thinks the dog winces
when her verbs are in the wrong tense.
She worries he'll mistake her frustration
with words for anger. She watches him
from the back door as he wanders
near the fence, and praises him,
bueno, bueno, when he comes back.

Siéntate—the galgo responds
to the familiar, not formal.
Can she learn a new language
from a dog? Anything seems possible
as he sits neatly before her,
his slender body, black and silver,
bred to run.

Jagannath

His statue's in the corner of the stage
at the odissi performance, his black body
draped in many-coloured cloth, and at the intermission
my sister-in-law whispers, *Who's that funny guy?*
I tell her it's Lord Jagannath, and she replies,
How do you know?

How could I not know Jagannath, having seen him
in temples since I was a child, having danced before him myself?
The Lord of the Universe has no arms or legs, no waist
or neck. His eyes are huge white circles outlined in red.

His name's become our English *juggernaut*.
At the annual festival in Puri, devotees who've come to celebrate
are sometimes crushed under his chariot's wooden wheels.
Even things that bring us together can move us toward
destruction. In a Western auditorium
far from India's eastern coast, we watch a woman dance.
The woman beside me, whom I call *sister*,
will soon be severed from my life.

Playing Dice with God

Science can only be created by those who are thoroughly imbued with the aspiration toward truth and understanding. This source of feeling, however, springs from the sphere of religion. . . . I cannot conceive of a genuine scientist without that profound faith.
–Albert Einstein

When I look through this microscope and see
the cytoskeleton and organelles of this single cell, I believe

that if I inquire deeply enough, I can come to understand
their innumerable complex functions. Is this not the nature of faith?

When I visit the observatory and examine distant planets
revolving according to laws I have studied, I think of Newton

and his neat equations, the same terms describing both
the falling apple and the orbiting earth. Is this not the beauty of science?

Dr. Einstein, it turns out that spooky action is real. We can
entangle quantum particles, and determine their wave function.

We can be sure of our uncertainty. The world we know
is unpredictable. God does play dice, and we can join him.

Kangaroo Conservation
for Professor Hartley Rogers, Jr., who taught me calculus

Travelling through the universe, I begin to wonder:
does one kangaroo plus one kangaroo equal two?
And what is the remainder
when dividing a kanga by its roo?

Can I calculate the integral
with respect to time
of a kangaroo from joey to adult
in its kangaroo prime?

How about the derivatives
of this same kangaroo—
what variables are correct?
What would Hartley Rogers do?

What are the implications if
two kangaroos collide?
Elastic or fully plastic?
Could theory alone decide?

Newton says for every force
there is an equal one opposed,
but only in classical mechanics
will a kangaroo stay composed.

In a quantum sense, who can say
how a kangaroo behaves?
Discretely, like a particle,
or interfering, like a wave?

If a kangaroo were inside a box,
would it be dead or alive?
Both states at once, Schrödinger says,
until we see inside.

Isn't it true the closer we get
to finding where he might be,
the further we are from knowing
his precise kangaroo speed?

And will this kangaroo travelling very, very fast,
seem massive, look slimmer, and appear never to grow old?
At such high speeds my intuition
never seems to hold.

In the continuum of time and space
we rarely see eye to eye,
but when we don't agree on the time we had tea
he doesn't seem to mind.

Come, my darling kangaroo,
hop out of your box, sip tea with me.
How beautiful the universe is
the more we uncover its mysteries!

It is no mystery, I suppose,
that nature's laws are always true,
though one thing I still don't understand
is this curious kangaroo, who,

in defiance of physics, I think, will try
to don a cape and learn to fly.

(And of these rhymes, this strange display,
what would Professor Rogers say?
"It's intuitively obvious
that your kangaroo needs a sleigh.")

Still Life with Tapers

for Grandma and Grandpa Harrison

They weren't my grandparents. Even if
mine were alive, they'd have been half a world away,
in India. My friend Katherine's grandparents lived
just an hour out of town. We spent a few
weekends there each semester, leaving Boston behind
but taking our books to study in their floral-upholstered living room
overlooking Nantucket Sound. She never called
to tell them we were coming. We walked

from the bus stop, six lefts and four rights,
and always found her grandfather working in the garage
while her grandmother rested inside after lunch.
They never let on that our visit surprised them. We settled in
as if we'd both grown up in that house; we knew
which rooms were ours. I graded chemistry problem sets
lying on my belly on the living room sofa,
my arm hanging down to the papers on the floor.

I called them Grandma and Grandpa, as if they, too,
were mine. She cooked, and he loaded the plates
into the dishwasher afterward. He checked for emails
while she typed letters on her typewriter, though
it was getting harder, she said, to find replacement ribbons.
At suppertime, she laid out his pills on the edge of his placemat
and lit the tapers on the table, the one on her left
before the one on her right. I can still see,

as if from my place beside her, the embroidered cloth
and twin glass candlesticks, the candle on the left
always shorter than the other. Her hand sure
but trembling.

Synapse

I once held a human brain.

I was visiting a friend
who studied neuroscience
at Stanford. In his lab, he lifted a brain
from a bucket of formaldehyde
and set its wrinkled mass
in the bowl of my latex palms.

Its clefts and recesses
called out to be admired,
opened up and fully known.
What currents and chemistries
once travelled these channels? What wisdom
pulsed through this small space?
How to calculate a surface integral,
program in C, stitch a wound,
or conduct a Mahler symphony?
How to speak Wolof, mend a shoe,
or construct a shelter out of snow?
Had this brain, alive inside a body,
travelled to China,
suffered from Crohn's,
danced to the beat of the djembe,
or scolded rowdy grandchildren stomping mud
across a newly scrubbed kitchen floor?
At the end, did it linger,
weakened by tumours or starvation,
or did it know trauma and smoke, a sudden
light then dark?

I slipped it back,
among its companions,

into the acrid solution.
My friend pressed down the lid.
I peeled off the thin gloves
and dropped them, inside
out, into the trash.

Seamus Heaney

After racking my oar, I ran straight
from the boathouse, took the T to Harvard, ran again
through the Yard and into the standing-room-only auditorium.
My legs too tired to stand, I sat on the floor, leaning against
the last row of seats with my back to the stage. I never
even glimpsed him, but his quiet brogue
reached through the hush to all of us. I can't say
how long I listened—*All I know is a door into the dark*—
but I can recall, anytime,
the sound of his voice: bottomless, humble, and unafraid.
It was a fall evening, the world outside was dark,
and his voice, the light.

Cosmology

for my husband

We used to think love
was easy to find. We were quarks
in the first femtoseconds
of the universe.

Bound by nothing, unaware
of broken
symmetries around us,

we were drawn together
by forces we could not understand.
Light scattered
in every direction.

We held each other tightly, a nucleus
of the smallest element.

Electrons bound. Atoms condensed
into quasars, luminous
and all-consuming. Dust
collapsed into fiery stars, radiating
energy, populating the ether
with heat.

We could not say what led to
this place. From where this cold
and darkness.

Ice and rock smashed together
and created bigger rocks. We found
ourselves in the curved arm
of a barred spiral galaxy,
on a molten planet orbiting a dwarf star.

Bombarded by the past, it took time
for molecules to form
membranes and cells, little rooms
where life could begin.

We learned to catch the light,
to make food and breathable air.

We learned to breathe,
to open our eyes and see
the earth that we evolved beside.
We learned to make music.

We used to think love was easy to find.
Now we know
the universe expands
from an unchangeable beginning
to an unknowable end.
Dark energy is impossible to define.

What we know sustains us:

You know this poem
is narrow because
I wrote it on a bookmark.

I know it was you who found it
covered in illegible marks
on the floor beside our bed
because you saved it
on my desk
for me to find in the morning.

The First Time

We started this leg of our trip in Mysore,
picked up at our hotel and driven up dusty roads
into the Western Ghats. I held my hand over my nose
and mouth for the journey, but when we arrived
the air was clean and cool. On a tour of the plantation,
our guide told us the Latin names of all the orchids in bloom.
She pointed out clusters of coffee berries, red and ripe, ready
for harvest. At dinnertime, we met our fellow guests—
from Switzerland, Denmark, and Austria, plus
a honeymooning couple from Bangalore—and ate our meal,
our delicious, simple, homegrown, home-cooked meal,
then talked until the stars appeared, so many, many stars.

At dawn, I awoke to a chattering of birds, so many,
many birds. It was the coolest morning I'd known yet in India.
Outside our room had been placed a thermos of hot coffee,
already mixed with milk and a bit of sugar. It reminded me
of the tea I'd grown up drinking, which is to say,
it was the first time I enjoyed the bitter taste of coffee.

Robert Pinsky

Passengers going to Hoboken, change trains
at Summit. Even in his crib, he considered
the rhythm of speech; as a boy, he studied
the drumming of sound. He would fiddle
with the saxophone for a time but later
find melodies in syntax. *Passengers going*
to Hoboken, change trains at Summit . . .

On stage in Ottawa, Pinsky's no longer
larger than life. He presses his palms together
before and after he speaks. He stretches his arms
to show the length of lines, holds up fingers
to count syllables. His memory amazes me.
I turn words inside out, he says, and
I believe him. I even watch him do it.
He turns the library's herringbone floor
into a poem about Cajun migration.

Truth is, I never liked his poetry much.
But I enjoy the man. He doesn't lecture.
He makes the afternoon light with stories.
I laugh to learn of his boyhood reverie,
hearing the conductor's drone, *Passengers going*
to Hoboken, change trains at Summit—his hand
moves up and down as he speaks—so rapt he'd forget
where he was going, forget to get off the train.

Save Our Stories

At the children's museum, I show the kids
how to dial a rotary phone: to place a fingertip
into a numbered circle, push clockwise, then release
and listen to its pulse back into place.
Around the corner, I'm hoping for a card catalogue,
to pull open its narrow drawers and feel
the imprinted letters, little ghosts
on the back of each typewritten card.

At home, my daughter knows how to save
her story—she clicks the blue-and-white square
in the top-left corner of the screen. She doesn't know
it's the image of a floppy disk, an object she's never seen.
She's never printed on paper with perforated edges
or tuned the radio by adjusting a fine, red line.

She'll never know the tricks of our time:
how we called home collect from a pay phone after a flight
and gave the wrong name—a code—so our parents
could reject the charges and know we were safe
without spending two dimes. How we hung the receiver
snug in its cradle, smug as tiny Pluto
holding its own among the giants
beyond the asteroids.

John Sharp Cromeans

When his belongings were
divided, only a book
came to me:
A French-English Dictionary
for Chemists.

Knowing that *grenouille*
means not only *frog,*
but also *a triturator*
for antimony sulfide,

makes me miss him
even more.

Coming Home in the Rain

I came home drenched, raincoat dripping, toes cold,
and there on the floor, where I'd be sure to see it,

a note, reminding me of that little thing I'd been trying all morning
not to let slip my mind, such a small thing I'm embarrassed

to mention it here. But there it was, your note, embellished
with butterflies you'd drawn around the words *Don't forget!*

carefully folded and weighted down so it wouldn't drift away.
I admit to being annoyed when I first saw it, the child in me adamant,

"I wasn't going to forget!" But those butterflies in blue marker,
floating your message to me, even in the rain. I thought of

how far monarchs travel, each generation carrying on the journey
of the one before. How each one knows, by instinct, where to fly

and where and when to stop and make a home. I felt a glimmer
of your love for me, even as I grumbled and kicked off my boots.

Mid-Life

You have grey hairs in your beard
and wrinkles at the corners of your eyes.

Our niece is getting married next week.
We talk of having another child.

I have been learning to play the piano:
it seemed impossible at first, though I dreamt

of effortless sonatas. Soon I could play scales
and knew without looking

when to raise a finger to a sharp or flat.
The first time I moved both hands

simultaneously in different directions,
every note I played was wrong.

I must make time to practice every day,
especially on these days that pass

whether or not we notice.
Has it already been fifteen years?

When you speak, the waves of your voice
touch the smallest bones in my body,

vibrating them like strings.

Nathan Cirillo

It is harder to lose something
when you know its name. See how easily
we can lose entire forests, when we live
in the city and never speak to those trees?
And how much joy from a bird we recognize—
a blue jay, say, or a cardinal—as a flash
of colour pauses to land on a rooftop.
When I heard of the murder
of a soldier downtown, I thought of only
my children at first: whether they
were safe at school, or alone, or afraid.
I thought of my husband's commute
that evening, how long it would take
for him to come home. I followed the news,
the photos of paramedics, noted
which streets were closed, which buses
were rerouted. But when they released
his name, Corporal Nathan Cirillo,
I felt my chest crumble. I walked outside
along my street and named the trees:
the maple, the ginkgo biloba, the ash
destroyed from the inside
by the emerald borer.

Immortality

We are walking to the library
because we live close by, and because
the morning is fine: we wear sweaters, not coats,
and the leaves still on the trees fleck the sky with gold.

My two-year-old holds my hand, and as we wait
for the crosswalk light to signal us safely across,
a squirrel hesitates in the middle of the street
and is smashed by a brown Mercedes.

As we'd watched him bounce along the grass,
my daughter called, "Squirrel! Come play with us!"
but now only the fur of his tail waves in the wind,
his guts are smeared along the pavement,
and one paw reaches up in perpetual plea.

"What happened to the squirrel?"

As I fumble words about death and the importance
of looking both ways before crossing the street,
I imagine the words of other mothers, and think
how the cares and admonitions of life
change with place and time. Why
playmates disappear, why the ground sometimes trembles,
and why, if you are hungry, it is okay to steal
mushrooms from the edge of a guarded field.
How there are so many ways to die.
Even things that sustain life vary with time:
Primo Levi wrote how forty hard rods of iron-cerium,
each twenty-five millimetres long, could be shaped
into one hundred and twenty cigarette lighter flints
and sold for four months' bread rations,
four months of life in Auschwitz. This morning,

I stirred a spoonful of honey into my tea
and consumed the life's work of twelve bees.
I think of Borges, and how he pictured
Paradise as a kind of library. How right he was,
not only because I would happily spend
eternity among books, but because
libraries are where we might live forever:
Shakespeare and Sappho coexist
with Ridley and O'Meara, who write in my city today.

We're approaching the library now,
and through the windows I can see
more books than I could read in my lifetime.
My daughter skips on the sidewalk and sings
a song of her own creation.

Nuchal Hand

What were you afraid of?
There are many ways to be born.

Why did you hesitate? Even a small gift,
barely the weight of a summer melon, comes with a cost.

I knew you would grow to love me—the folds of skin
on my knuckles, my tapered nail beds and curve of wrist—

and at night, I know, you will think of me:

How I tore through you, when you decided to submit.
How quickly pain ends, when work is done.
How details desire to be noticed. They must.

You did not need me in order to learn these lessons,
but I was there. You yourself created me.

Frenulum of Tongue

By now, you must know
the power of small,

hidden things. Tucked
beneath, I can spread

teeth, make speech
indecipherable. Even

milk, modest
and adored,

I can clamp
until my demands

are met. Do not
forget: I, too,

am your creation.
Martyr me, if

you must. Make me
immortal.

Scaphocephaly

And then, after all that,
after your most raw delivery,
and the baby's frenectomy,
and the five-year-old's head lice,
and the nine-year-old's birthday party,
and breastfeeding, and diapering,
and laundry, and laundry, and laundry,
the doctor said, *Your eight-week-old*
needs an ultrasound of her head.

In the days between the referral
and the appointment at the Children's Hospital,
you learned how to move slowly. As
if that would be enough. When the neuro-
surgeon asked, *If I told you your baby needed*
an operation, would you run away screaming
and never come back? you told him you were ready
for anything, because you knew you had to be.

It was summer, spacious and warm. You made tea
every morning in a quiet house. The sun rose; the trees
carried on their steady endeavours. The phone rang.
It turned out her sagittal suture showed no sign
of premature fusion. Everything was normal.
But from then on, how you held her extra close.

Let Me Tell You a Story

Because everyone said she looked like her father,
because she had his height and sense of humour
and I knew she'd inherited his gentleness and caution,
when she, eleven years old, took the floor
to present the story she'd rehearsed for weeks
behind her closed bedroom door, having carefully
planned her outfit down to her socks and brushed her hair to a dark sheen,
I was startled to behold my eldest daughter, and in her body, me.

Saṃsāra

We planted your placenta under a peach tree;
your sister's went under the tomatoes in our new garden.
We didn't want to leave it in the care of strangers, so
the peach sapling we put on a friend's farm.

Your sister's went under the tomatoes in our new garden.
That first year, the tomatoes were prolific.
The peach sapling we put on a friend's farm
because we were leaving our old house that same month.

That first year, the tomatoes were prolific.
We had more than we could eat; even the squirrels got fat.
Because we were leaving our old house that same month,
we knew we'd never taste the peach tree's fruit.

We had more than we could eat. Even the squirrels got fat.
After that, we had everything we could want, though
we knew we'd never taste the peach tree's fruit.
We did not plan to return to the land of your birth.

After that, we had everything we could want, though
we didn't want to leave it in the care of strangers.
We did not plan to return to the land of your birth, so
we planted your placenta under a peach tree.

Dung Beetles

It takes tenacity to survive on others' shit.
To fly into a fresh pile, still steaming,
to break off a piece and roll it
into a ball for easy transport. To roll it
backwards, with head to the ground,
blind to rocks or holes in the road. It takes
geometry to roll it in a straight line, always
a straight line. A famous poet once told me
the best poems are non-linear, but a straight line
is the quickest escape from would-be thieves.
Thieves abound in the chaos of the mound, so the male
beetle rolls his ball away, as straight and as far
as he can. If a rock bars his path, he moves around it,
then continues to roll. If he falls from a height, he climbs
atop his ball and dances, then continues to roll. At night,
never mind the lack of polarized skylight. Under the new moon,
dung beetles roll their balls in straight lines. Never mind their tiny
dorsal eyes, too poor to resolve particular stars. The steady
brushstroke of the Milky Way is visible even to a beetle
rolling a ball of dung. Never mind poetry's non-linear logic:
it takes faith to navigate by a galaxy.

Ritual

Since I don't believe in life after death,
I cling to this life: to the china teacups, fragile
and imperfect, demanding my deliberate love.
Since I don't believe in a personal god, I hold fast
to ritual: to morning walks in darkness, past the stonecutters
with their broad shoulders, hardened from years of bringing down
mountains; and past the soothsayers, calling on believers
to come and hear their fortunes. They cry out as I pass,
ever hopeful for a convert. But I don't believe in conversion, only
transformation: the sun's rising ever later as winter comes,
the teacup's shattering as it hits the spinning earth.

Free Fall

A glass dropped from a height will shatter.
Without support, it will succumb
to gravity,
which is everywhere,
and all at once. Can you feel it?
Sometimes it is difficult for me to even get out of bed.

I am helping my children make a card for my father.
They are laughing, remembering Parcheesi games
and banana cakes. I watch them practice Malayalam letters—
the characters I taught them as he taught me—
before they copy them onto his card. They are planning
the pictures they will draw for him, and my tears
are falling to the floor.

My Mother Never Speaks Her Fears

Once, when I was swimming,
my body panicked, and my mind
splintered and fled. I turned to kick
to the surface, but water surrounded me, laughing
with all its glittering faces. I could see bright lights
on the far-off ceiling, but there was always
a film over my face. One, two, how many
kicks did it take before I broke
through, breathing hard through my mouth.
For days afterward I imagined dying
a hundred different ways.

Today, I watch my mother spoon-feeding
her husband of fifty-six years. Dad is ninety-two.
I'd imagined death as fire or falling, or being trapped
in a beeping hospital room, but never
like this: at home, the quiet. Daddy never speaks
of his own dying but asks Mom why she is so sad,
as she weeps while asking him to open his mouth.

My Father Comes to Me in a Dream

I sit at a small, round table
in front of a window overflowing
with light. A young man
slides into the chair beside me.
"I know a way to escape," he says.

It is unmistakably my father, younger
than I have ever known him. His hair
is oiled and combed. He is dapper
in a red sweater. I do not realize,
until that moment, that I am trapped
inside a column of light—above
and below and behind me is all aglow—
but I am not alarmed or afraid.
I am overjoyed to be with my father.
There is no one else who knows me.

My Husband Asks If I Am Sad

and I say no. I am hollow, like a drum. Tap my belly
and you will hear an expansive noise, like thunder.
Submerge me in water, and I will fill up and sink.

I am a tree with an empty space in its trunk,
which could be a home for some living thing, but
I am afraid to reach my arm into the dark.

Little Song from the Kitchen Table

Hot chilies, green beans, eggplants, and tomatoes
that you would weed and water every day
grew there, along the house, in careful rows
edging the backyard where I used to play.
The tendrils of the bitter gourd would grip
the wires of the kitchen window screen,
and I uncurled their dainty fingertips
while Mom chopped vegetables for our next meal.
Now, unplanted beds are such a mess,
grown over with grass and unruly weeds,
and overlooking these—Daddy, forgive me—
this morning I mentioned to the hospice nurse
that you loved to garden. You are here,
and today I spoke of you in the past tense.

I Invoke My Father's Ghost

He does not whisper in my ear or jump
out from the shadows. He uses my mouth
as his mouth. He grunts and cackles
nonsense sounds with an Indian tongue.
My children can hear him, but they are not
afraid. They tell me I am too silly to be
a mom. I do not tell them I am possessed.
He is in my mind, but I do not mind. He is
not dead, but I have summoned his spirit
for company. Sometimes when my throat
conjures sounds particularly like his
—oh, the funny syllables he used to sing!—
the children laugh, and I taste my own blood.

I Think of Dad While Buying a Sandwich

He always knew what it would be: BLT.
Never checked the menu, just asked, BLT?
I can still hear his voice, how he pronounced BLT.

It was the first sandwich he ever bought, a BLT.
In a new country, it was easy for him to say BLT.
After that, it was the only sandwich he ever bought, a BLT.

If Dad were here, he'd be asking for a BLT.
There are things that sound better to me than BLT,
but Dad will be here if I order a BLT.

Sing Me an Indian Song

In the early morning darkness of our room,
sunlight merely edging the closed blinds,
her unexpected voice, unexpectedly sweet,
without demand or expectation, only hope,
asked for something that, in our household,
in her life, only I could give. I snuggled close
and sang a *bhajan*, a devotional song, the song
my family and I sang in the last moments that
my father's body remained intact on this earth.
I thought of my father while I sang in Malayalam
for my youngest daughter, his namesake. Joy
rushed toward me from every hidden corner.

Frost Flowers

Rootless, they require no soil. Their seeds
are imperfections on the surface of the sea.

They bloom when temperatures plummet,
and disappear, sometimes, within hours.

If I could speak a native Arctic tongue, I would
have told you this in the space of a single breath.

They suck salt from the ocean. I could hold one in my mouth.
By the thousands, they release aerosols that alter polar atmospheres.

Their crystalline hollows, abundant with bacteria,
are home to more life than the sea ice beneath them.

If I could convey in words the splendour of such small things,
I would not be afraid of living such a short time.

NOTES

This book's epigraph is from Carole Glasser Langille's poem "Plough" from her book *Church of the Exquisite Panic: The Ophelia Poems*.

Of the various sources I consulted for the poem "Elementary Particles," I am particularly indebted to Frank Wilczek's essay "A Piece of Magic: The Dirac Equation" from *It Must Be Beautiful: Great Equations of Modern Science*, edited by Graham Farmelo. Greek words and definitions are from the Online Etymology Dictionary, www.etymonline.com.

"To Thousand Island" owes a debt to Kenneth Koch's book *New Addresses*.

"My *Ramayana*" references the 1987-88 TV series *Ramayan*, starring Arun Govil as Ram.

The Pablo Neruda epigraph for "Four" is a translation by William O'Daly, and the Big Bird quotation is from the song "I Just Adore Four," written for *Sesame Street* by Sam Pottle and Joseph A. Bailey.

The epigraph for "Taxicab Numbers" is from G. H. Hardy's book *Ramanujan: Twelve Lectures on Subjects Suggested by His Life and Work*.

"Playing Dice with God" makes reference to two well-known Einstein quotations. "God does not play dice with the universe" is how Einstein expressed his view that the randomness and probabilities of quantum mechanics must be the manifestation of underlying deterministic laws. He was famously skeptical of the idea of quantum entanglement, a phenomenon in which entangled particles seem to instantaneously affect each other even if they are far apart; Einstein called this "spooky action at a distance." The poem's epigraph is from the essay "Science and Religion," which is collected in Einstein's book *Ideas and Opinions.*

The italicized phrase in "Seamus Heaney" is the first line of Heaney's poem "The Forge" from his *Opened Ground: Selected Poems 1966-1996.*

Nathan Cirillo was a Canadian soldier who was fatally shot on October 22, 2014, while on ceremonial sentry duty at the National War Memorial in Ottawa. The opening sentence of "Nathan Cirillo" is a paraphrase of a remark made by Patrick Lane during an Ottawa International Writers Festival event two days later.

The story of how iron-cerium rods were converted to bread rations in Auschwitz, referenced in "Immortality," is found in Primo Levi's autobiographical essay "Cerium" from his book *The Periodic Table.*

The structure of "Let Me Tell You a Story" is inspired by that of Matt Rader's poem "Leave the Light On" from his book *A Doctor Pedalled Her Bicycle Over the River Arno.*

"Ritual" grew from a prompt to use first lines of other poems as inspiration. The first line of "Ritual" comes from a poem whose title and author I have forgotten. I offer the author my apologies and appreciation. "Ritual" also takes inspiration from the first line of Michael Ondaatje's poem "The Medieval Coast" from his book *Handwriting.*

ACKNOWLEDGEMENTS

Thank you to everyone at Brick Books, particularly Alayna Munce, Brenda Leifso, and my editor, Cara-Lyn Morgan, for guiding this book into the world with patience and care. Thank you to Emma Allain for focusing my vague idea for a cover into an elegant book design.

Many thanks to the editors and teams at the publications in which poems from this collection previously appeared:

"Rosa Parks" won *Arc Poetry Magazine*'s Diana Brebner Prize in 2015, was selected for *The Best Canadian Poetry in English 2016*, and was reprinted by *Arc* in 2022 to celebrate the 20th anniversary of the Diana Brebner Prize. "Rosa Parks" was also printed on a poster and hung in various downtown locations in March 2021 as part of Ottawa Poet Laureate Deanna Young's "Poems for Ottawa" project.

"Thoppil Bhasi" and "Robert Pinsky" were shortlisted for the 2015 Montreal International Poetry Prize and published in *Global Poetry Anthology 2015*.

The suite of "Frost Flowers," "Etymology," and "Cosmology," published in *The New Quarterly*, received an honourable mention at the 2018 National Magazine Awards. An extra thank-you to the editors of *TNQ* for selecting my work for submission to the NMAs.

"Four," "Save Our Stories," "Synapse," and "Taxicab Numbers" were originally published in my chapbook *Variations in Gravity*. My thanks to D. S. Stymeist for producing this beautiful, hand-bound chapbook through Textualis Press.

Other poems from this collection first appeared in *The Antigonish Review, AUIS Literary Journal, CV2, Event, The Fiddlehead, Grain, New Contrast, Ottawater, Rabbit Poetry Journal, Rattle,* and *Room.* Some poems were reprinted in the League of Canadian Poets' Poetry Pause and in the above/ground press chapbook anthology *Bodies and Breath.*

I am grateful to the Ontario Arts Council and the City of Ottawa for grants that supported the writing of this book, and to the Canada Council for the Arts for a travel grant to attend the Banff Centre's Writing with Style residency in September 2014.

Thank you to Lorna Crozier, for her mentorship at the Banff Centre, where the beginnings of this manuscript emerged, and for her ongoing guidance and encouragement.

Thank you to the vibrant and close-knit community of writers in Ottawa; I appreciate you all, more than you know. Thanks especially to David O'Meara, for his generous feedback on an early version of this manuscript, and to the members of my writing group, the Ruby Tuesdays, for inspiration, support, feedback, and friendship.

Thank you to my mother, for her unwavering support and enthusiasm for my writing. To my beloved father, thank you for everything, especially for instilling in me a love for both science and language. I miss you every day.

Deepest gratitude to my husband, John. This book would not exist without your love and support. And to our daughters, Anasuya, Shailaja, and Dhanya. Everything I write is for you.

Sneha Madhavan-Reese was born in Detroit and now lives with her family in Ottawa. She has degrees in mechanical engineering from MIT and the University of Michigan. Her writing has appeared in publications around the world, including *The Best Canadian Poetry in English 2016*. She serves on the editorial board of *Canthius* magazine, and is the author of one previous poetry collection, *Observing the Moon*.